DATE DUE			

921
PON

Manning, Ruth.

11367

Juan Ponce de Leon

615014 01795   19371D   057

Juan Ponce de León

Ruth Manning

Heinemann Library
Chicago, Illinois

©2001 Reed Educational & Professional Publishing
Published by Heinemann Library,
an imprint of Reed Educational & Professional Publishing,
100 N. LaSalle, Suite 1010
Chicago, IL 60602
Customer Service 888-454-2279
Visit our website at www.heinemannlibrary.com

Designed by Wilkinson Design

Printed by Wing King Tong, in Hong Kong

05 04 03 02 01
10 9 8 7 6 5 4 3 2 1

Library of Congress Cataloging-in-Publication Data
Manning, Ruth.
    Juan Ponce de Leon / Ruth Manning.
        p. cm. -- (Groundbreakers)
    Includes bibliographical references and index.
    Summary: Describes the life of the Spanish explorer who first came to the new world
with Columbus and went on to become governor of Puerto Rico and later came to Florida
looking for the Fountain of Youth.
    ISBN 1-57572-376-X
        1. Ponce de Lean, Juan, 1460?-1521--Juvenile literature. 2.
    Explorers--America--Biography--Juvenile literature. 3.
    Explorers--Spain--Biography--Juvenile literature. 4. America--Discovery and
    exploration--Spanish--Juvenile literature. [1. Ponce de Lean, Juan, 1460?-1521. 2.
    Explorers. 3. America--Discovery and exploration--Spanish.] I. Title. II. Series.
    E125.P7 F67 2000
    972.9'02'092--dc21   00-029561
    [B]

Acknowledgments   The publisher would like to thank the following for permission to reproduce photographs: The Granger Collection, pp. 4, 11, 20, 22, 26, 32, 34, 35, 40; North Wind Pictures, pp. 5, 6, 15, 17, 27, 36, 37; Library of Congress, pp. 19; Stock Montage, pp. 9, 10, 14, 18, 22; Museum of Mankind, London, UK/The Bridgeman Art Library, p. 16; Pierpont Morgan Library, p. 21; Robert Frerck/Odyssey, pp. 24, 38, 41; Corbis, pp. 25, 28, 39; Andre Jenny/International Stock, p. 29; Corbis/National Museum of Natural History, p. 30; Mary Evans Picture Library, p. 31; Super Stock, p. 33.

Cover photograph: The Granger Collection

Some words are shown in bold, **like this.**
You can find out what they mean by looking in the glossary.

Contents

Florida—and a Fountain of Youth?

Man of many achievements

Juan Ponce de León is known primarily for two reasons. He was the first European to discover and name Florida. He is also supposed to have searched for the **Fountain of Youth,** a magical fountain he heard about from the Caribbean people. Whoever drank the waters from this fountain would not grow old. Instead, they would become young again.

We know, however, that Ponce de León did far more than these two things. Historians think he probably fought against the **Moors** who ruled in southern Spain in the fifteenth century. He was also probably one of the people who sailed with Christopher Columbus on his second voyage to the New World. He played an important role in the history of Hispaniola—the island that is now home to Haiti and the Dominican Republic—and **Borinquen.** It took courage to sail to this New World that had just been discovered. The land was in unknown territory, and maps of the area were just being drawn.

El Adelantado IUAN PONCE *Descubridor de la Florida.*

Ponce de León gained fame for his adventures in the Caribbean Sea and in Florida.

FACTS

The New World
When Ponce de León sailed with Columbus, he probably thought that he was going to India or China to bring back the spices and wealth to be found there. No one knew what to expect on such a voyage. It took courage to go into the unknown.

A fountain of youth?

Did Ponce de León believe in the Fountain of Youth? Some historians say that he didn't, but that he used the fountain as an argument to look for new territory. The king he served, King Ferdinand of Spain, was in his sixties—an old man in those days. He was probably excited at the possibility of becoming young again.

The story of a magic fountain had been around since the time when Alexander the Great explored new territory in the fourth century B.C. At that time, legend said that the fountain was in Asia and was fed by the waters of the Garden of Eden. Another story located the fountain in a kingdom beyond the known world. It was said to be ruled by Prester John, a Christian king. No one had ever seen Prester John, but he was widely believed to exist. So, when Christopher Columbus announced that the fountain was somewhere between the island of Trinidad and the northeast coast of Venezuela, people tried to find it again.

The fifteenth and sixteenth centuries were an exciting time in Europe. So much new information about the world was being discovered that ideas about how the world looked and what existed in it were always changing. At this time, finding a fountain of youth was an important scientific goal, because people thought it would contain a cure for old age.

To leave the safety of the coast and sail the open sea was to risk storms and monsters, according to the beliefs of the fifteenth century.

An Age of Exploration

Ignorance about the world

Early maps show us that people in Europe knew only a small part of the world. Those who built the **empires** of Alexander and Rome explored by land or the coasts, never going too far from shore. According to fantastic tales of the time, the open seas were filled with terrifying sea monsters and the dangers of the end of the world. Still, the **Vikings,** from Scandinavia, set sail in their boats to travel across the north Atlantic. They told many stories of their voyages, but did not leave behind maps. Physical evidence of their presence in the New World is just now being found.

What motivated the Europeans to start exploring? Merchants wanted to find new places to buy and sell, and new routes by which to ship their goods. **Crusaders** wanted to spread Christianity. Rulers wanted power over new lands to protect their **empires** at home. They wanted to explore territories rich in gold and slaves. A new spirit arose as Europe recovered from the devastation of the Black Plague—a terrible disease that killed almost one-third of the population. People shared new ideas as the Renaissance—the era of new learning—spread from Italy to other parts of Europe.

This map was made just before Columbus's discovery of the New World in 1492.

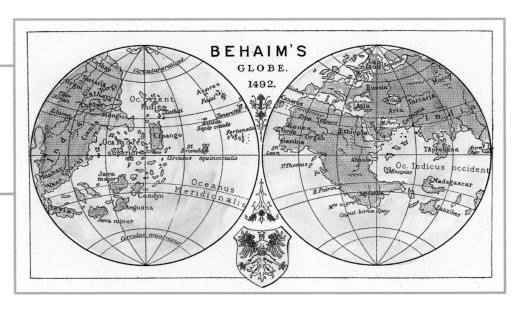

Portugal and Spain

Although small in area, Portugal played a large role in the explorations of the fifteenth and sixteenth centuries. Unlike Spain, Portugal had become an independent country in the mid-1200s. It no longer had to fight invaders from outside the country, so its rulers could turn their attention to other matters, such as exploration. Because Portugal's long coastline lay on the Atlantic Ocean, the Portuguese began exploring areas near their coast. Prince Henry the Navigator, who studied geography and **navigation,** sponsored many of Portugal's expeditions. He believed it was possible to reach India by sailing around Africa. India was an important source of jewels, rugs, silks, spices, and other goods. Beginning with Morocco in 1415, the Portuguese traded and **colonized** along the African coast and the islands of the Atlantic. Then, in 1498, Vasco da Gama became the first European to sail around the southern tip of Africa and reach India. This sea route became one of the most important trade routes for Portuguese sailors.

Spain was not originally a unified country like it is today. Several small kingdoms held control of the land. Before they could think about exploring new territory, Spain's rulers first had to unite these kingdoms and then defeat the **Moors.** Finally, in 1492, the king and queen of Spain could turn their attention away from their own land. They sent Christopher Columbus to find a fast and easy route to India. Instead he found the New World, and the era of Spanish exploration began.

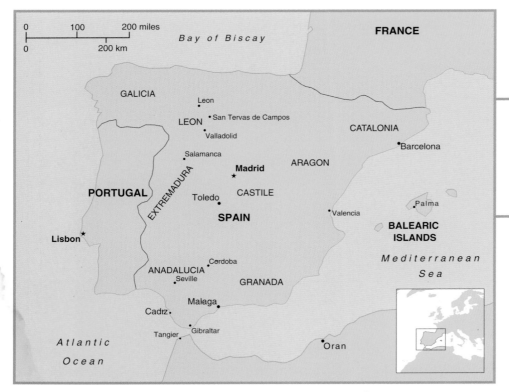

The provinces of Castile and Aragon united in 1469, forming the powerful new nation of Spain.

Unknown facts

No formal records of Ponce de León's birth have been found. Most references give the date as 1460. However, historians have found a record of his testimony in a court case in 1514, in which he gave his age as forty. If the testimony is true, that would mean that Juan Ponce de León was actually born in 1474.

Although he came from a distinguished **noble** family, Ponce de León's mother and father are unknown. His parents may not have been married. Important members of the Ponce de León family lived around the Spanish cities of Seville and Cádiz. **Don** Rodrigo Ponce de León was a leader in the wars of Granada against the **Moors.** Don Pedro Ponce de León was the duke of Cádiz in 1492.

However, Juan Ponce de León was probably from the part of the family from the north of Spain. He was born in San Tervas de Campos, on the right bank of the Valderaduey River, not far from the city of Valladolid. As a boy, he was sent to be trained as a **page** in the household of Pedro Núñez de Guzmán, a distinguished noble.

The coat of arms of the Ponce family and the training Juan received indicate that he probably was from a noble family.

Training to be a knight

Ponce de León lived in a time when the best education for a boy was to be trained as a **knight.** Núñez de Guzmán may not have been the wealthiest Spaniard, but his status and ability to train young men were well known. He was asked to educate members of the royal family.

As a page, young Ponce de León served as a personal servant to Núñez de Guzmán in return for being taught how to ride a horse, fight, and hunt. He was expected to learn social graces and manners. Either his **tutor** or a priest taught him about the Roman Catholic faith. He probably also learned to read and write.

When he was fourteen or fifteen, his training shifted to preparing to fight in battles and tournaments. He had the status of a **squire** and was expected to accompany his knight into war. He would have been expected to protect his master or to hold the knight's horse. He may have participated in the battle against the Moors for Granada—either as a squire or a knight, depending on his age at the time.

It is possible that Ponce de León's first taste of warfare occurred in the battle of Granada in 1492.

FACTS

Armor
The suits of armor that the knights wore had to be designed for protection and for ease of attack. Good armor was expensive and had to be kept in good condition.

Isabella and Ferdinand

Warfare

In Spain, the **knights** served their lords, and their lords served the king and queen. A problem for the lords who lived in Castile—one of the provinces of what is now Spain—was figuring out who the king and queen were. The king of Castile had no children, so he made his half-sister, Isabella, his **heir.** However, Isabella married Ferdinand of Aragon—another province—without her half-brother's permission. The king no longer considered Isabella to be his **successor.**

Ferdinand of Aragon became king of Castile when he was only 22, and king of Aragon at the age of 27.

Isabella and Ferdinand married for political reasons. They wanted to join the two provinces and unite the small kingdoms that controlled the land occupied by Spain and Portugal. They fought to gain or keep control of Castile and Aragon from 1475 to 1479. They then entered into ten years of war against the kingdom of Granada to throw out the **Moors,** who had entered Spain from Africa in the eighth century.

At the end of this war, Isabella and Ferdinand had a large army trained in European warfare. This included using tactics such as paying soldiers by allowing them to **loot,** using attack dogs, and holding leaders for **ransom**. In Ponce de León's time these tactics were considered normal. When Spanish soldiers went to the New World, they brought these tactics with them.

Isabella's reign

Isabella was a remarkable woman for her time. She was interested in warfare. She was responsible for improvements in methods of supply and the establishment of a military hospital. She brought scholars to her court to teach her **Latin.** Isabella created a new palace school for the sons of the **nobles,** and she encouraged art.

She was a **devout** Roman Catholic who was concerned with the quality of the people appointed to church offices by the **pope.** Although the pope had granted Isabella and Ferdinand the title of the "Catholic Kings," Isabella did not hesitate to oppose the pope if she did not agree with his choices or if she thought he was taking power that she had traditionally held over the churches. During her reign, the **Inquisition** forced thousands of non-Christians, especially Jews, to flee Spain. Christians who disagreed with the Church's official teachings were also targets of the Inquisition. Those who stayed in Spain risked torture and even execution for disagreeing with the teachings of the Roman Catholic Church.

Isabella of Castile ruled most of Spain from 1474 until her death in 1504.

However, Isabella is perhaps best remembered for her approval of Christopher Columbus's voyage to sail west in search of India. Her support helped make the discovery of the New World possible.

Christopher Columbus

News of the New World

Columbus affected the life of Ponce de León in two ways. First, the exciting stories Columbus brought back with him may have made Ponce de León decide to leave Spain to try his luck in the New World. Second, the ship on which Ponce de León traveled to the New World was part of the fleet that Columbus led on his second voyage.

Excitement ran through Isabella's court when Columbus returned in 1493 with news of the land he had found by sailing west. He had brought back a little gold, some people he called Indians, and some colorful birds. Isabella was not happy with the way the Indians had been treated. She ordered some Indians that Columbus had brought as slaves to be freed. Yet she and King Ferdinand treated Columbus with great honor when he returned. If Columbus had found a new route to the **Indies**, which would bring wealth to Spain through trading, then many of Spain's unemployed soldiers could hope for a future fortune from the New World. Ponce de León was chosen to sail with Columbus on his second voyage.

When Columbus returned from the New World, Isabella and Ferdinand gave him a grand reception in Barcelona.

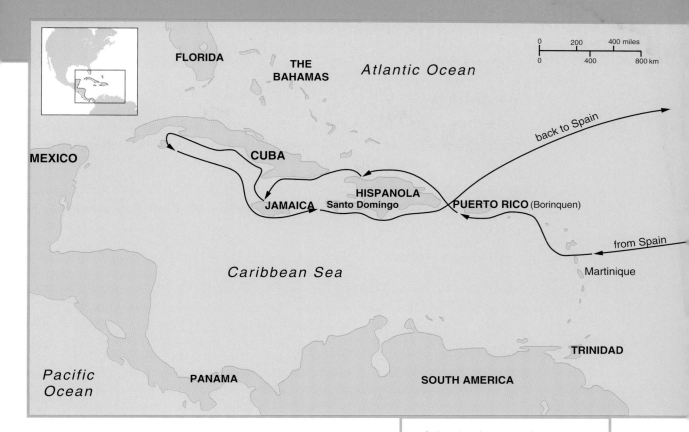

Second voyage of Columbus

Columbus was at the peak of his popularity when he left Spain on September 25, 1493, with at least seventeen ships. Plans to establish a colony and bring Christianity to the Indians were part of this trip. He had about 1,300 paid men, perhaps 200 private **investors,** a small troop of **cavalry,** and a group of Roman Catholic priests.

Columbus's second voyage to the New World took a southern route. With good winds, he arrived in a little over a month.

The trip across the Atlantic went fairly quickly. They reached one of the Caribbean islands, Dominica, on November 3. The fleet sailed past what are now known as the Virgin Islands and entered the Samana Bay in Hispaniola—present-day Haiti and the Dominican Republic.

Here, Columbus discovered that the people he had left behind on his first voyage had died. Either they had died of natural causes or they had been killed by the Indians. Their fort had been destroyed. Some of the Indians were fighting the newcomers to their land. Columbus established forts and founded a city that he named La Isabella, after the queen. Ponce de León may have served as a soldier in one of these places.

Conquest of Hispaniola

Colonization

Columbus had brought several hundred people with him to settle the lands of the New World. However, many of them were more interested in finding gold than in planting crops. They immediately started hunting for gold fields and were discouraged when they were unable to find large quantities of gold in time to return to Spain on the next ship. They did not want to build a town in the New World.

Before Columbus sailed off to further explore the Caribbean, he left a man in charge of conquering and patrolling the island. This man tried to take power from a council that Columbus had established. When he was unsuccessful, he took the first ship back to Spain before Columbus could return from his trip, leaving the colony in chaos.

Some of what we know about this period comes from a biography of Christopher Columbus written by his son, Hernando. In his book, Hernando reported that many Spanish soldiers robbed and mistreated the Indians they met, especially the women. Sometimes **missionary** priests would try to protect the Indians, but they were not always successful. Many of the Indians responded with violence against the Spaniards.

Columbus named the island he found "Hispaniola," meaning "Spanish Island."

Ponce de León's role

Ponce de León's name first appears in written history in a report that was written by Bartolome de Las Casas, the first Roman Catholic priest **ordained** in the Americas. According to Las Casas's account, Ponce de León sailed with Columbus, not as one of the "gentlemen of the land" who would have been given land and slaves, but as a foot soldier. As a soldier, he would have had to protect the Spaniards and fight against the Indians.

Reports by de Las Casas, and later by a Spanish governor, record the Spaniards' cruelty to—and even torture of—the Indians on Hispaniola. No one is sure if Ponce de León was involved. Some historians have suggested that he was not in Hispaniola at this time but had returned to Spain. However, no evidence has turned up in Spain of his presence there. A report has been found from 1502 that lists Ponce de León as a captain of the Spanish forces at Santo Domingo. This promotion probably means that he was good at his work.

The site of La Isabella was probably chosen because it was close to a source of gold, but it was poorly located for good water, soil, or port access. It was also in an area with many mosquitoes, which spread disease.

The Inhabitants of the Caribbean

Who were the Indians?

The people that fought against Ponce de León and his troops were a mixed group. When Columbus reached the shores of the West **Indies** in 1492, there were about six million Native Americans living there. There were three distinct groups—the Ciboney, the Arawak, and the Carib. Except for a few small populations in Dominica, Cuba, and Puerto Rico today, these groups have largely disappeared. The first people in the area probably came from Central America sometime between 5000 and 2000 B.C. They hunted animals and gathered fruit and other food. Then, about 1000 to 500 B.C., the Ciboney moved in from South America. They had pottery and tools that were different from those used by the earlier peoples.

Around 300 B.C., the Arawak came to South America and settled on Trinidad and other islands. There must have been thousands on Hispaniola. They lived in villages in circular houses. The villages were ruled by chiefs. The Arawak planted crops and had fine fabrics, gold ornaments, and pottery.

The Carib came from Venezuela around 1000 A.D. They were an aggressive group with fine canoes and cloth. They built villages in places where they would be protected from surprise attacks.

The Arawak were skilled carvers, using both wood and stone. Some of their carvings have survived to this day.

The view of the Spaniards

Several Spaniards from Columbus's second voyage wrote down their impressions of the people they found in the New World. One of these sources is a letter written by a man named Chanca, who was the expedition's doctor. He wrote that the Indians walked around as "naked as their mothers bore them," covering themselves only with belts made of woven cotton, or with grass or leaves. To a Spaniard used to the heavy, elaborate clothing of the day, this must have seemed odd, and maybe even shocking.

Dr. Chanca was also interested to note that the Indians painted their faces black, red, or white, and partially shaved their heads in intricate patterns. He wrote that he and many of the Spaniards found this very odd.

This 1594 picture of cannibalism shows the European's horror of this custom.

In addition to describing the Indians' appearance, Dr. Chanca also wrote about their behavior. He reported that they often raided other islands and took all the women they could, especially the young and beautiful ones. The women were taken to serve as wives and servants of the raiders. However, he said that the Carib warriors ate all the male children that they had by these servant women, and only let the babies born to women of their own tribe live. As for the men they captured, "they bring those who are alive home to be slaughtered and eat those who are dead on the spot." They let the boys live and took them home to be servants, but killed and ate them after they became adults. Our word cannibal comes from the Spanish name for the Carib Indians.

Ponce de León's Life on Hispaniola

Marriage and a home

By 1502, Ponce de León was living in Santo Domingo, the main Spanish settlement on Hispaniola. Here he met and married his first wife, Lenore. She may have been the daughter of an innkeeper in Santo Domingo. In Spain, a person from this social level would not have been a very good match for a young **noble.** However, she was Spanish, not a native, and she had a **dowry.** These qualities made her a desirable wife in the New World. She and Ponce de León had four children—Juana, María, Isabel, and Luis.

Ponce de León's new social status as a married man and his skill as a soldier were rewarded in 1504. In that year, Nicolas de Ovando, the governor of Hispaniola, named Ponce de León provincial governor of Higuey, an area on the eastern part of the island. Ponce de León built a large stone house in Salvaleón—the only house of its kind in the province. This showed that he intended to stay on Hispaniola. People who planned to return to Spain or move on to other places in the Spanish empire were content to live in less permanent houses made of mud and straw.

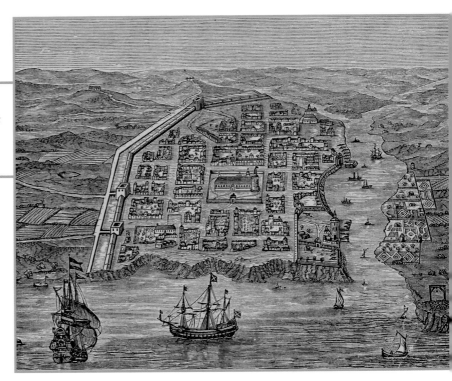

Santo Domingo was founded by Columbus's brother Bartholomew in 1496.

Indian revolt

Part of the reason for the governor's recognition of Ponce de León came from his effective service in putting down a native **revolt.** The Indians in the province of Higuey decided that they would no longer put up with the Spaniards' demands for food, gold, and women. They captured a Spanish fortress and killed nine of the ten men who were stationed there.

Ovando, the governor, organized a force of about 300 Spaniards, together with some of the other friendly Indians, to go to Higuey. The Indians there fought with arrows, rocks, and clubs, but the Spaniards had horses, dogs, swords, and protective armor. The revolt ended with the capture and public execution of the chief. Many of the Indians fled to the mountains or other islands. Others surrendered to the Spaniards to become laborers on their farms.

This engraving shows an Arawak chief trying to defend a hill in the mountains of Hispaniola against a Spanish attack.

The province assigned to Ponce de León was not popular with the Spaniards because the Indians had told them it contained little gold. However, it was a good land for growing crops such as bananas, mangoes, and sugar cane. Ponce de León, on orders from the governor, built two towns there—Salvaleón and Santa Cruz de Aycayagua.

Spanish Colonial System

Division of land and slaves

How did the Spaniards carve up the land they had conquered? Settlers were given land in both the town and country. Town lots were for the construction of housing. Country lots of about 33 acres (13 hectares) were for farming.

However, the Spaniards did not expect to do the work themselves. Each settler received between 30 and 80 Native American Indians to work as house servants or farm laborers. The Spanish **nobles** received more than the commoners, and married men received more than bachelors.

D. FR. BARTHOLOME DE LAS CASAS
Del Orden de Predicadores, Obispo de Chiapa Varon apostolico, y el mas zeloso de la felicidad de los Indios.
Nació en Sevilla el año de 1474, y murió en Madrid de 1566.

*Bartolome de Las Casas was a Dominican **missionary** and historian. He was known as "the **Apostle** of the **Indies**" because he spoke out against the Spaniards' cruelty to the Indians.*

Unfortunately, many of those people who first settled in Hispaniola did not stay. Some returned to Spain. However, most of those who moved went to other parts of the Spanish New World. The news of gold and silver from Panama and Mexico caused many people to look for wealthier and easier spots to start a new life.

Although the Indians were often mistreated, the priests who were sent to **convert** and teach the Indians sometimes tried to protect them. Bartolome de Las Casas was one who fought to change the evils he saw. He and others discussed the moral and legal problems of conquest and rule, which resulted in the **Leyes Nuevas** ("new laws") of 1542. While these legal protections of the Native American Indians were often ignored, no other European countries had such laws.

Agriculture

The Spaniards were pleased to find that the land of Hispaniola was good for farming. In his book about his father, Hernando Columbus wrote that the climate of Hispaniola was not too different from that of Spain, "being cool rather than hot." The temperature stayed between 60°F (16°C) and 90°F (32°C) for most of the year. The rains of the islands, which were cold, light, and good for growth, were also similar to those in Spain.

Hernando reported that the land on Hispaniola was so fertile that grape seeds sprouted within a week, and unripe grapes could be gathered in three weeks. The land and climate were ideal for growing crops such as oranges, rice, tobacco, and avocadoes. According to Hernando, Columbus was "delighted with the nature of the climate, and with the fertility and people of the country."

Ponce de León developed a large farm that he devoted to raising food crops, cattle, and horses. He intended to stay. However, he was also aware that the Indians traded with others on an island named **Borinquen** that lay 80 miles (130 kilometers) east of his settlement. This island would be the site of his next adventure.

The Arawak tended gardens with several types of grain and food-bearing plants. They hunted fish with bows and arrows and also used nets.

Exploration

The Indians on Hispaniola told Ponce de León about the gold on the island to the east. He reported this to his governor, Ovando, who ordered him to investigate. Ships had stopped at the western end of the island to get water. But no one knew what the land away from the coast was like.

In 1506, Ponce de León set sail for the island with five ships and about 200 men. He landed at the western end of the island and discovered that Arawak lived there. The Arawak feared the Carib, who lived at the eastern end of **Borinquen**. The Spaniards promised to help the Arawak defeat their enemy. Ponce de León sent some of the ships back to Ovando with some gold. He then established locations for mines and set the Indians to work gaining more of this precious metal. Then, all of the Spaniards returned to Hispaniola with more gold.

Because of the success of the exploration, Ponce de León was ordered to return and settle the island. In 1508, he returned to settle the island with just one ship and 50 men. The ship nearly sank when two great storms drove it against the rocks.

The Arawak used baskets to gather gold from streams and rivers.

Travel could be dangerous in the Caribbean Sea, an area known for its violent storms.

Administration

Ponce de León established a home at Caparra, a settlement near the present capital of San Juan. It was not as grand a home as on Hispaniola, having only white-washed mud walls, but it did have **fortifications** around it. He divided the land and Indians the way it had been done on Hispaniola and began the mining and farming that were needed to bring in money.

Ponce de León was expected to pay all the expenses, including food and supplies for the laborers. The king took one-fifth of the gold that was mined. The remainder was divided between the king and Ponce de León. Although the king had the best of the bargain, Ponce de León came out of the project a wealthy man. Also, he established a **foundry** for the **refining** of gold in Caparra.

The Indians were awed at first by the power of the Spaniards and believed them to be **immortal.** However, before long they decided that they had endured enough of the mistreatment from some of the Spaniards. They rebelled against one of the worst of the offenders. Ponce de León commanded the forces that put down the **rebellion.**

Colonial Politics

Claims of Diego Columbus

Nicolas de Ovando, governor of Hispaniola, had made Ponce de León governor of the island of **Borinquen**. However, Christopher Columbus had died in 1506. Diego, his son and **heir,** was trying to establish his right to the promises that had been made to his father. The king had removed the Columbus family from any government positions in the New World because of problems that family members had created in the past.

But Diego wanted what had been promised to his father before his first voyage. Diego had become powerful through his marriage to a woman from an important Spanish family. The courts decided that he only had the right to govern lands that Christopher Columbus had actually discovered—not all of the Spanish New World.

Unfortunately for Ponce de León, those lands included Borinquen. In 1511, by order of the king, Diego Columbus replaced Ponce de León as governor.

Diego Columbus built this Columbus Palace in Santo Domingo, Hispaniola, in 1523.

Casa Blanca ("White House") was built in the 1520s by Ponce de León's family and was the home of his descendants for over 250 years. It is the oldest house in Puerto Rico.

Consequences for Ponce de León

Because Ponce de León had been appointed by the previous governor, Diego Columbus saw him as a rival. Therefore, he put in place two men who were loyal to him—Juan Ceron and Miguel Diaz, whom Ponce de León had once had jailed.

Ceron and Diaz now controlled the assignment of lands and people. Ponce de León and his friends were not treated fairly. The two new administrators did not know how to handle the people, the agriculture, or the mining. Much of what Ponce de León had accomplished was destroyed.

Meanwhile, Ovando, the previous governor, had returned to Spain. He and Pedro Núñez de Guzmán—whom Ponce de León had once served as a **page**—spoke to the king on behalf of their friend. The king did not want Ponce de León hurt by the rights he had been forced by Spanish politics to give to Diego Columbus. However, Ponce de León did have some of his land, his stone house on Hispaniola, and one of his ships taken away. For a time, he was under house arrest, meaning that although he was not put in prison, he was not allowed to leave his house. Although Ponce de León continued to be the highest military authority on Borinquen and had certain other honors, the situation must have been unpleasant for him. He was ready to look for new lands to conquer.

Search for Bimini

Why Bimini?

The Spaniards explored new land in search of gold and slaves. If those ideas about a **fountain of youth** proved true, so much the better. Who could object to the idea of eternal youth?

In order for a Spaniard to be able to profit from the discovery of a new land, he first had to get permission from the king. Thus, Ponce de León applied for and was granted a **contract** to look for an island called Bimini. He was given the title of **Adelantado,** which meant that he had to equip and finance the voyage himself. Then he would be able to use the land he discovered for his own profit. One advantage of Bimini was that the Columbus family had no claims on it. The king was able to reward Ponce de León in a way that he could not on **Borinquen**.

Ponce de León may have actually believed in the Fountain of Youth, or he may have used it as a way of getting approval for his expedition.

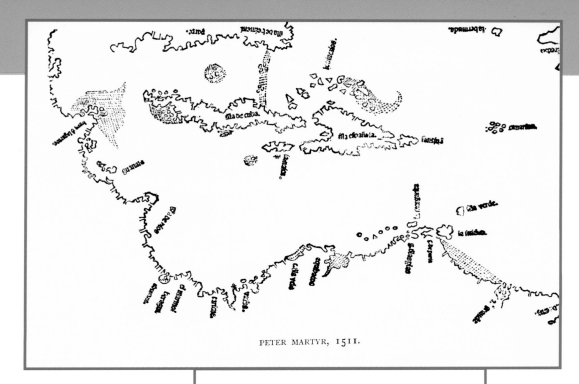

PETER MARTYR, 1511.

Peter Martyr's 1511 map was based on reports from men on Spanish ships.

Where was Bimini?

Bimini is now the name of a group of small islands in the Bahamas. However, in 1512, when Ponce de León was granted his contract, Bimini was thought to be a large island about 975 miles (1570 kilometers) from Hispaniola.

Peter Martyr, who was then secretary to the **Council of the Indies,** mentioned this fact in a report to the **pope** that included information on the Fountain of Youth. Even more significant is Martyr's map of the islands and shoreline of the New World, published in 1511. The information he used to draw the maps came from oral and written reports passed on to him by **navigators** from Spanish ships. On the map is a long shoreline drawn to the north of Cuba that he labeled "isla de beimeni parte" (island of Bimini). The Grand Bahamas are next to the land mass, and what might be interpreted as the Florida Keys are at the lower end.

With such a map already in existence, is it likely that Ponce de León was really the first European to discover Florida? It is possible that ships seeking fresh water or slaves could have stopped in Florida. The unfriendly reception Ponce de León received from the Indians might suggest it.

Preparations and first landing

On March 3, 1513, Ponce de León left Anasco Bay on the western side of Puerto Rico with three ships—two **caravels** and a **brigantine.** He was looking for new islands. He did not know that Florida was a peninsula attached to a large continent. About thirty sailors and thirty soldiers and farmers sailed with him. One man brought his wife and her sister. Two Native American slaves were on board as guides. There were also two free blacks on the crew. These men probably came to the New World as slaves of Spaniards, who later gave them their freedom.

Experienced men captained the ships. The pilot, Antón de Alaminos, set a northwest course through or around the Bahamas. The strong Gulf Stream current carried them more north than west. They first anchored in 44 feet (13.4 meters) of water in a point thought to be south of what is now Cape Canaveral, near Melbourne Beach.

When Ponce de León went ashore to claim the land for Spain, he found trees and flowers on flat, even gound. He landed on April 2, during the Easter season. Because the Spaniards called Easter the "Feast of Flowers," Ponce de León named the land "La Florida," from a Spanish word meaning "flowery."

YOU CAN FOLLOW PONCE DE LEON'S VOYAGE ON THE MAP ON PAGE 42.

It would not be surprising if the Spaniards tasted the Florida waters—just in case they could regain their youth.

Contact with the inhabitants

After five or six days at the first landing site without any contact with Indians, Ponce de León sailed south. On April 21, he made another discovery—the force of the Florida current, or Gulf Stream—at a cape north of the Lake Worth Inlet. Two of their ships were carried backward, and the brigantine was pushed out to deep water. Because they had sighted Indians, Ponce de León and his men anchored north of this cape and rowed to shore.

Ponce de León had hoped for a friendly meeting, but the Indians attacked with clubs and arrows and wounded three sailors. Stopping at Jupiter Inlet for firewood and water, Ponce de León was attacked by a larger party of sixty men. He took one of these men as prisoner to be a guide. Then, staying close to shore, he went south to Key Biscayne and Key West. He turned west, landed on the Gulf Coast at San Carlos Bay, and anchored at Sanibel Island. Here, he met with more hostile people. One Spaniard and three Indians were killed.

> On their route back to Borinquen, Ponce de León's ships made stops at three Florida keys.

Ponce de León decided to turn back to **Borinquen.** On the way, they stopped at a few small islands where the crews stocked their ships with land and sea animals, including 160 loggerhead turtles. These islands are now called "Las Tortugas," from the Spanish word for turtle. Two of the three ships arrived at Borinquen in mid-October. The third ship was still looking for Bimini. The crew found a wooded island but no sign of the **Fountain of Youth.** They returned four months later and claimed that Bimini had been found. The island they found, however, was probably Andros.

Destruction of the Calusa

At the time of the Spanish expedition, the Calusa nation controlled the southwestern part of Florida. Their capital city, called Calos, was built on a huge mound of shells. It was located in the area of San Carlos Bay, near what is now Fort Meyers. Although the Calusa were successful in driving away Ponce de León, diseases brought by the Europeans soon killed many of them. This may have ended the power of the chief.

Resources were plentiful for the Calusa. The sea provided them with large quantities of marine life. They even developed **lagoons** for harvesting oysters and stone pens for turtles and fish. They did not farm the land, but they hunted animals and gathered roots and wild fruit.

In 1895, wood carvings were found submerged in the swampy area at Key Marcos—a condition that preserved the wood from the Calusa culture.

The Calusa traded with the inhabitants of the nearby islands. They sailed in double canoes fastened together. They were equipped with sails and carried as many as fifty persons.

Since food was easy to find, the Calusa had time to produce fine artwork. Their wood carvings are considered to be some of the finest to come from the Native Americans of North America. Many of these fragile wood objects that have survived to this day were preserved in a swampy area at Key Marco. They were discovered in 1895.

Change in the Spanish sea routes

Because of the discovery of the Gulf Stream on this first voyage, there was a shift in the sea route for gold being sent to Spain. Antón Alaminos, the chief pilot of Ponce de León's voyage, was working for Hernán Cortés, the conqueror of Mexico. Cortés wanted to send a great present of gold to the Spanish king, but he was afraid that pirates would capture the ship.

Alaminos recalled the fight that he had with the Gulf Stream on his earlier voyage and advised Cortés that this current might be a good new route to Spain. He took his treasure ship from Mexico to Havana through the Florida Straits and sailed north along the east coast of Florida until he was opposite of Bermuda. Then, he turned his ship east across the Atlantic Ocean and headed to the port of Cádiz in Spain.

Because of the new sea route for the gold shipments, the main port in the West **Indies** shifted from Santo Domingo, on Hispaniola, to Havana, Cuba. For a while, the pirates were outsmarted.

During the time of Ponce de León, pirates were a big problem in the Caribbean. Most of them tried to rob the ships that were sending gold back to Spain.

FACTS

The Calusa
The Calusa chief was believed to have supernatural powers. At his capital he could entertain 2,000 guests. The Calusa even built islands from mounds of shells with sea walls and wind breaks. The fifty-acre (20-hectare) island at Key Marco had nine canals, several lagoons, and an 18-foot (5.5-meter) pyramid mound temple. The central court had water tanks and terraced gardens. Many carved masks and ornaments have been found here.

Return to Spain

In order to register his new discoveries with the king and keep others from presenting a prior claim, Ponce de León went back to Spain. He wanted to present his **petition** to the king so he could obtain official permission to proceed with settlement of the new land.

His former master, Pedro Núñez de Guzmán, had an important position at the court of the king. He was able to get Ponce de León a chance to meet with the king. The king must have been pleased with his report, because Ponce de León was given a new **contract** for the settlement of Florida.

Ponce de León was made a **knight** and given a personal coat of arms. The coat of arms showed three islands in sea waves on a field of blue representing **Borinquen**, Florida, and Bimini, with an uncrowned red lion (león) on a silver background. The contract entitled him to be called **Adelantado.** The knighthood meant that he would have the title **don** before his name. In official documents, he was now called "The Adelantado don Juan Ponce de León, Governor of the Island of Bimini and Florida."

Seville in 16th century Spain was the rich city where ships assembled for expeditions.

Orders to fight the Carib

The king had received complaints of raids by the Carib on the island of Guadeloupe in the West **Indies**, as well as on Borinquen. Because Ponce de León had a reputation for successfully fighting the Carib when he was governor, the king ordered him to go to Seville, the city in Spain where expeditions were organized. He was instructed to prepare an expedition against the Carib before proceeding with settlement plans. He was told to do this "at the least cost that can be." Spain was not yet receiving gold from Mexico and Peru, and the small quantities that arrived from Hispaniola and Borinquen were not enough for all of the expeditions being planned.

Ponce de León sailed from Spain with his expedition in 1514. When he reached Guadeloupe, he sent ashore a small guard of soldiers and some women to wash sheets and shirts. In a surprise attack, a group of Carib captured or killed this landing party and then retreated to the forests of the island. Without native guides or trained dogs, pursuit was useless, so Ponce de León had to sail on to Borinquen. No further raids took place on Borinquen. Ponce de León concentrated on defending that island rather than launching a new attack on Guadeloupe.

Stone piers in the harbor near old San Juan in Puerto Rico were built by the Spaniards in the fifteenth century.

33

Return to Spain

A new king and new information about Florida

King Ferdinand died in 1516. His grandson Charles came to power, bringing with him a group of advisers who were not Spanish. The new king was known as Charles I of Spain and Charles V of the **Holy Roman Empire,** his larger European territory. To make sure that this new king would protect his interests, Ponce de León planned a trip to Spain to meet him.

Several other Spanish expeditions had stopped at Florida since Ponce de León's trip to obtain slaves or supplies. On one of these, in 1519, Alaminos, the chief pilot for Alonzo Alvarez de Pineda, discovered that Florida was not an island but a peninsula. Pineda noted where Florida joined on the western coast and named a river the Rio de Espiritu Santo, meaning "River of the Holy Spirit." The river might have been the Mobile River, the Mississippi River, or the Louisiana River.

Ponce de León, who had not been back to Florida in eight years, needed to take action on his plans to settle his discovered land. In 1521, he wrote to Charles that he planned to establish a settlement there.

El Greco's famous painting of Toledo shows a typical Spanish city of the sixteenth century. Adjusting from the Old World to the New must have been difficult for many explorers.

Personal worries

In 1512, Ponce de León had been ordered to pay a large sum of gold to the Royal Treasury by the judge who reviewed his work as governor of **Borinquen**. The judge also had refused an **appeal.** However, when the judge retired, Ponce de León had another chance to file a complaint in this matter. He won his case in 1520, at which time the fine was paid back to him. He now had extra money. The case is important because the court papers give many of the dates and details of his life.

Also, sometime before his trip back to Spain in 1516, Ponce de León's wife died. When he returned to Spain for an eighteen-month stay between 1516 and 1518, he married his second wife, Juana Pineda. His new father-in-law filed a lawsuit against him in a dispute about his daughter's **dowry.** His second wife died before he set off on his second expedition to Florida in 1521. By that time, his son was settled in Santo Domingo, and his daughters were married.

Charles V became Holy Roman Emperor when he was only nineteen.

FACTS

Charles of Spain

While Charles was to have a long reign and was able to consolidate his power and add to his territory, Ponce de León met with his king when the king was young and new to Spain. Would this young man want to continue the policies of his grandfather, King Ferdinand? Would Charles recognize the **contract** with Ponce de León that Ferdinand had granted? Ponce de León had good reasons for concern.

Attempted Settlement of Florida

Second voyage to Florida, 1521

On February 26, Ponce de León sailed from **Borinquen** in two ships that were loaded with 200 settlers, parish priests, and missionaries, as well as 50 horses, livestock, and seeds. The author Fernandez de Oviedo, a personal friend of Ponce de León, reports in his history: "And as a good settler he took with him, mares, calves, swine [pigs], sheep, goats, and all manner of domestic animals useful to the service of man. Also for agriculture and working the fields there were provided all [kinds of] seeds; as if the business of its [Florida's] settlement was nothing more than to arrive and cultivate the land and pasture his cattle."

However, life was not that simple. Oviedo reports that the climate of the region was not the same as Ponce de León had expected. Southern Florida is very hot and humid during the summer months. Also, he found that the Indians were fierce fighters who were not pleased by the idea of giving up their land to these bearded strangers from across the sea.

YOU CAN FOLLOW PONCE DE LEON'S VOYAGE ON THE MAP ON PAGE 43.

The second Florida expedition in 1521 was attacked by hostile Indians.

Unknown facts

Unfortunately, Ponce de León's second voyage is not well documented. No one is certain, but he probably landed in the same region that he had visited on his first trip—San Carlos Bay.

Oviedo reported that when they landed, Ponce de León gave orders that the people should "rest themselves." Historians are not sure where this resting period took place or how long it lasted. Did people actually start building a settlement? According to Oviedo's account, a **missionary** effort may have been attempted with the Indians.

Ponce de León's expedition met with a hostile reception. Historians are not sure whether the Indians attacked in one big battle, or if there were a number of **skirmishes.** What is known is that in one attack, Ponce de León was seriously wounded in the thigh. He ordered the ships and the settlers to return to Cuba.

Ponce de León's men carried him back to the ship.

FACTS

How Was Ponce de León Wounded?
We do not even know that he was wounded in a land battle. Some writers have noted that because the Indians were such skilled sailors, a lucky arrow shot could have wounded Ponce de León while he was on board his ship.

Death and the Future

Ponce de León's expedition

On the return to Cuba, one of the ships was blown off course in a storm. It eventually landed in Mexico where the supplies assisted Hernán Cortés, the conqueror of that territory. The other ship carrying the wounded and horses arrived in Cuba.

You can follow Ponce de Leon's voyage on the map on page 43.

Ponce de León's wound did not heal, and he died from an infection in July of 1521. When Ponce de León realized he was close to death, he appointed one of his group to take charge of his goods. This person was instructed to sell everything, use the money to buy horses, and take them to Mexico to sell. Ponce de León's **heirs** were to receive the profits.

Juan Ponce de León II, a grandson, transferred the remains of his famous ancestor from Havana, Cuba to the church of San José in San Juan, Puerto Rico. Historian Juan de Castellanos composed his **epitaph:**

"Here rest the bones of a Lion
    mightier in deeds than in name."

Ponce de León's body lay in this church for 300 years.

Spanish settlement of Florida

By 1520, Spain was using the name "La Florida" for the entire southeastern quarter of what is now the United States. Vazquez de Ayllon received authorization to settle on the "Land of Chicora." Chicora was the name of an Indian who spoke of the wonders of his homeland in what is now South Carolina. When Ayllon and 600 colonists arrived on these shores, they decided that it did not live up to the praise of the native. So they headed south to Georgia and on September 29, 1526, founded a town called San Miguel de Gualdape—the first named European settlement in what is now the United States. The Georgia settlement lasted for two months, and then the survivors went south to the islands of the West **Indies**.

This Georgia settlement was even earlier than those of Florida—Pensacola in 1559, Fort Caroline in 1564, and St. Augustine in 1565, although St. Augustine holds the record as the first permanent settlement. The settlement of Florida was a slow process. Other areas in the New World were more attractive—they had gold and fewer hostile Indians. Panfilo de Narvaez in 1528 and Hernando de Soto in 1539 marched through Florida in attempts to conquer the Indians. Their expeditions provided more information about this new territory that eventually became part of the United States.

In 1913, the body of Ponce de León was moved to San Juan cathedral from the church of San Jose, where it was placed in a marble tomb.

Ponce de León's Legacy

What he accomplished

Why is Juan Ponce de León important if he probably was not the first European to stand on Florida sand, and if he did not find the **Fountain of Youth?** The answer lies in what he did achieve during his life.

As a young child in a poor but **noble** family, he made his way in the world. Starting as a **page,** Ponce de León rose to be recognized by his king as a **knight.** He risked a trip to the New World on the second voyage of Christopher Columbus. As a soldier, he worked to take command. Instead of chasing the latest rumor of gold, he married and established a farm on Hispaniola and raised a family. Then, he explored **Borinquen**, founded cities there, and became governor. Although colonial politics caused his removal from power, he went on to be given authority to explore Florida and Bimini and later to **colonize** Florida. He died fulfilling his commitment to his king.

Ponce de León was honored in his home country by this postage stamp.

40

How he has been honored

Juan Ponce de León has been recognized in many geographic place names. His image has appeared on postage stamps. Because of the courage, curiosity, and perseverance of Juan Ponce de León, he has been recognized as one of the most important Europeans to explore the New World. He brought Spanish culture and religion to the places in which he established homes—now Haiti, the Dominican Republic, and Puerto Rico. Monuments to him can be found in Florida and Puerto Rico.

Although the tactics that he used against the Native Americans seem cruel to us now, they were common in the European wars and considered appropriate in his society. He greatly increased the Spaniards' knowledge about the New World. Without men like Juan Ponce de León who willingly risked their lives, exploration and colonization would have been impossible.

Memorials to Juan Ponce de León can be found throughout the Americas.

41

Maps

Historians and mapmakers have recreated Ponce de León's voyages in the New World. The map at the top of page 43 shows his first voyage to Florida in 1513. The map below it has been enlarged to show all the places Ponce de León explored in Florida. At the bottom of this page, the map shows his return voyage to Florida in 1521. Note that the red arrow showing Ponce de León's path veers off toward Cuba, where he died of wounds he received in Florida. The blue line shows the path of the other ship in that expedition, which was blown off course shortly after leaving Florida. The supplies it carried went to help Hernán Cortés's expedition in Mexico.

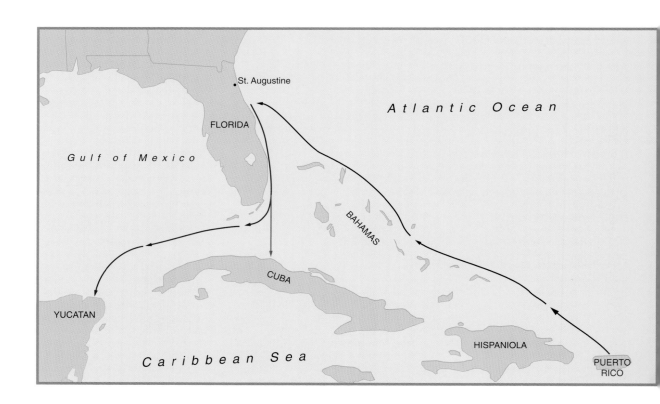

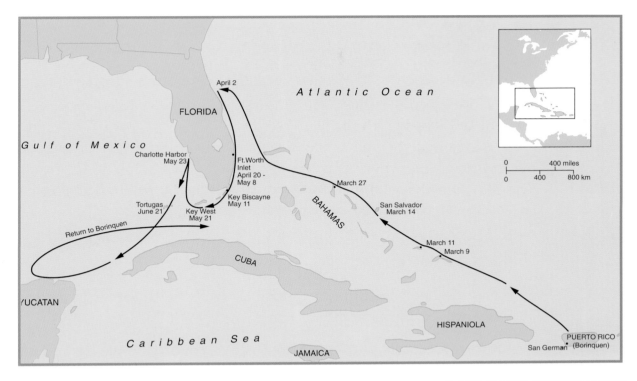

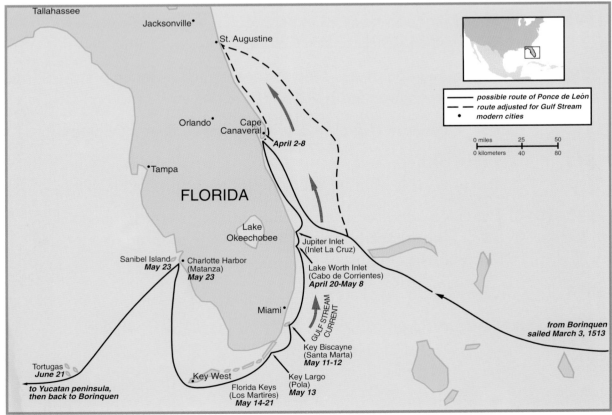

Timeline

1415	Portugal begins exploration and trading along African coast.
1460?	Date of birth traditionally assigned to Juan Ponce de León.
1469	Isabella of Castile marries Ferdinand of Aragon, uniting two large provinces to form Spain.
1482–1492	Isabella and Ferdinand fight against the kingdom of Granada to defeat the **Moors.**
1492	Christopher Columbus discovers the Americas while trying to find a way to India by sailing west.
1493	Ponce de León accompanies Columbus on his second voyage to the New World.
1502	Ponce de León becomes a captain of the Spanish forces at Santo Domingo on Hispaniola.
1504	After successfully putting down a native **revolt,** Ponce de León is made a deputy governor of the province where he lived.
1506	Ponce de León leads an expedition to explore the island of **Borinquen**. Christopher Columbus dies in Spain.
1508	Ponce de León makes second voyage to Borinquen to establish a settlement there and is appointed acting governor.
1511	Ponce de León is replaced as governor by Diego Columbus.
1513	Ponce de León sets out on first voyage to Florida and lands there, naming what he thought was an island "La Florida."
1513–1514	Ponce de León returns to Spain, where he is **knighted.** He is given a **contract** to settle Florida and is ordered to fight the Carib in Guadeloupe and Borinquen.
1516	Charles I becomes new king of Spain.
1516–1518	Ponce de León returns to Spain to meet the new king.

1519	Alaminos, chief pilot for Alonzo Alvarez de Pineda, establishes the fact that Florida is a peninsula, not an island.
1521	Ponce de León makes second voyage to Florida to establish a settlement but is wounded. He sails with his expedition to Cuba, where he dies.
1526	First settlement made in what is now the United States in South Carolina, by an expedition led by Vazquez de Ayllon.
1528	Panfilo de Navarez explores Florida.
1539	Hernando de Soto explores Florida.
1542	Spain adopts the **Leyes Nueves** of the **Indies** to give the Native Americans some legal protection.
1565	St. Augustine, Florida, is the first permanent settlement in what is now the United States.

More Books to Read

Cardona, Rodolfo, and James Cockcroft. *Juan Ponce de León: Spanish Explorer.* Broomall, Penn.: Chelsea House, 1995.

Heinrichs, Ann. *Florida.* Danbury, Conn.: Children's Press, 1998.

Morley, Jacqueline. *Exploring North America.* Lincolnwood, Ill.: NTC Contemporary Publishing Co., 1996.

Sanchez, Richard. *Spain: Explorers and Conquerors.* Minneapolis, Minn.: ABDO Publishing Company, 1994.

Glossary

Adelantado person authorized to explore and profit from a territory at the cost of equipping and financing the project

appeal strong request for help or a different decision

apostle person who spreads religious teachings or brings about great changes for religious reasons

Borinquen original name of the island now called Puerto Rico

brigantine ship with two masts and square sails

caravel small ship with three or four masts, used in the fifteenth and sixteenth centuries

cavalry soldiers mounted on horseback

colonize to settle a new territory

contract legal written agreement

convert to convince someone to join a religion

Council of the Indies Spanish council making decisions about the New World

crusaders European Christians who tried to take over the Holy Land from the Muslims during the middle ages

devout devoted to religion

don honorary title similar to "sir" in English

dowry property a woman brings to her husband in marriage

empire group of territories or people under one ruler

epitaph something carved on a person's tombstone in memory of them

fortifications something used to make a building safer or stronger, such as stone walls

foundry building or factory where metals are cast

Fountain of Youth magical fountain that would make people young again, thought to exist at the time of Ponce de León

heir someone who will inherit property or a title after the death of the owner

Holy Roman Empire empire lasting from the ninth through the eighteenth centuries, consisting mostly of German and Italian states and ruled by a single emperor

immortal able to live forever

Indies islands in the Caribbean Sea that early explorers mistakenly thought were part of Asia

Inquisition religious persecution in Spain of non-Christians

investor someone who puts money into a business or voyage and receives a share of the profits

investor someone who puts money into a business or voyage and receives a share of the profits

knight man who was given an honorary military rank and who pledged to fight for a lord or other ruler

lagoon shallow pond connected to a larger body of water

Latin language of ancient Rome that was the official language of the church

Leyes Nueves Spanish laws that tried to regulate the government of colonies in the New World

loot to rob or steal openly and by force, as during war

missionary someone who travels to another country to spread their religion

Moors Muslims from Northern Africa who conquered Spain in the eighth century

navigation science of figuring out the position and course of a ship

noble of high birth or rank, or a person of high rank

ordain to make a person a Christian minister or priest by a special ceremony

page in the Middle Ages, a boy in training to become a knight

petition to make a written request to someone in power, such as a king or queen

pope leader of the Roman Catholic Church

ransom money paid to free a person from captivity or punishment

rebellion open fight against the government, also called a revolt

refine to bring something, such as metal, to a pure state

Renaissance time in Europe of new discoveries and fresh interest in the ideas of the ancient Greeks and Romans, lasting from the fourteenth to the seventeenth century

revolt open fight against the government, also called a rebellion

skirmish small fight between two armies

squire person who carries the shield or armor of a knight

successor person who is next in line for a throne, title, or office

tutor person who teaches another, often one on one

Viking member of one of the Scandinavian tribes that invaded the coasts of Europe from the eighth to tenth centuries

Index